FORT SUMTER

Joanne Mattern

Rourke
Educational Media

rourkeeducationalmedia.com

Scan for Related Titles
and Teacher Resources

Before Reading:

Building Academic Vocabulary and Background Knowledge

Before reading a book, it is important to tap into what your child or students already know about the topic. This will help them develop their vocabulary, increase their reading comprehension, and make connections across the curriculum.

1. *Look at the cover of the book. What will this book be about?*
2. *What do you already know about the topic?*
3. *Let's study the Table of Contents. What will you learn about in the book's chapters?*
4. *What would you like to learn about this topic? Do you think you might learn about it from this book? Why or why not?*
5. *Use a reading journal to write about your knowledge of this topic. Record what you already know about the topic and what you hope to learn about the topic.*
6. *Read the book.*
7. *In your reading journal, record what you learned about the topic and your response to the book.*
8. *After reading the book complete the activities below.*

Content Area Vocabulary
Read the list. What do these words mean?

ammunition

barracks

battery

bombardment

Confederate

drilled

federal

inauguration

ironclads

plantations

seceded

Union

After Reading:

Comprehension and Extension Activity

After reading the book, work on the following questions with your child or students in order to check their level of reading comprehension and content mastery.

1. What was the purpose of raising the flags at Fort Sumter? (Inferring)
2. Why were some states seceding from the Union? (Summarize)
3. Why was slavery important in the South but not in the North? (Asking Questions)
4. Why was Fort Sumter built? How long was it under construction? (Summarize)
5. Why is Fort Sumter considered an important symbol of the Civil War? (Asking Questions)

Extension Activity

There were many flags flown during the Civil War. Research the different flags that were in the North and South. What were the major differences between them? How were they similar? Choose two flags and create a Venn diagram to address the differences and similarities of each. Could you reimagine our American flag today? What would it look like?

TABLE OF CONTENTS

Chapter 1

A NATION ON THE EDGE

In 1860 the United States had been a nation for less than one hundred years. During the 1770s, the thirteen British colonies had joined together to form a new nation made up of separate states. By 1860 that nation had grown to thirty-three states. However, it was not easy to get all those states to work together as one United States.

Each state had its own laws and way of doing things. The **federal**, or national, government also had laws. Sometimes, the state and federal laws did not agree. Different laws about slavery would cause the biggest problem the United States would ever face.

Slavery had existed in the United States since colonial days. But the northern states had gotten rid of slavery, while the states in the South had not. Southern states needed slaves to work on their **plantations** and allow them to produce goods such as cotton. The southern states also did not want other states to tell them what to do. As far as the South was concerned, they had every right to keep slaves.

Southern plantation owners relied on slaves to work on their huge plantations. The southern economy could not work without slaves.

By 1860 the issue of slavery was tearing the United States apart. That year Abraham Lincoln was elected president of the United States. Lincoln was against slavery. The southern states did not want Lincoln to change their way of life. So eleven of the southern states decided they did not want to be part of the United States anymore. They **seceded**, or left, and formed their own nation, called the Confederate States of America. That action began a long struggle called the Civil War.

When the Civil War began, Fort Sumter was an unfinished building in the harbor of Charleston, South Carolina. Over the next three years, this fort would become one of the most important symbols of the Civil War.

Abraham Lincoln (1809–1865)

The Confederate flag is also known as the "Stars and Bars" because of its design.

Fort Sumter

Union states without slavery
Union States with slavery
Confederate States
Territories

Robert Barnwell Rhett

In 1860 Robert Barnwell Rhett wrote in the *Charleston Mercury* newspaper: "There exists a great mistake...in supposing that the people of the United States are, or ever have been, one people. On the contrary, never did the sun shine on two peoples as thoroughly distinct as the people of the North and South."

*Robert Barnwell Rhett
(1800–1876)*

Chapter 2

FORTS IN THE HARBOR

Charleston, South Carolina, is located on the Atlantic Ocean. Ever since the first days of the United States, this city has been one of the most important ports in the country. For this reason, Charleston has always been protected by forts.

This marker, located in Charleston, South Carolina, chronicles the facts and events of this controversial time in history.

Americans built Charleston's first fort on Sullivan's Island during the Revolutionary War. The fort was named Fort Moultrie after its commander, William Moultrie. On June 28, 1776, nine British warships attacked Fort Moultrie. None of their shots hit the building. The Americans fired back and finally drove the British ships away.

After the Revolutionary War ended, Fort Moultrie fell apart. In 1798 another Fort Moultrie was built on the site of the original fort. The new fort had five sides. Its walls were made of mud and timber and rose 17 feet (5.2 meters) high. However, this new fort was no match for a hurricane which destroyed it in 1804. In 1811 another Fort Moultrie was built. After the United States faced the British again in the War of 1812, the young nation decided it needed a bigger and better fort to protect the Charleston Harbor.

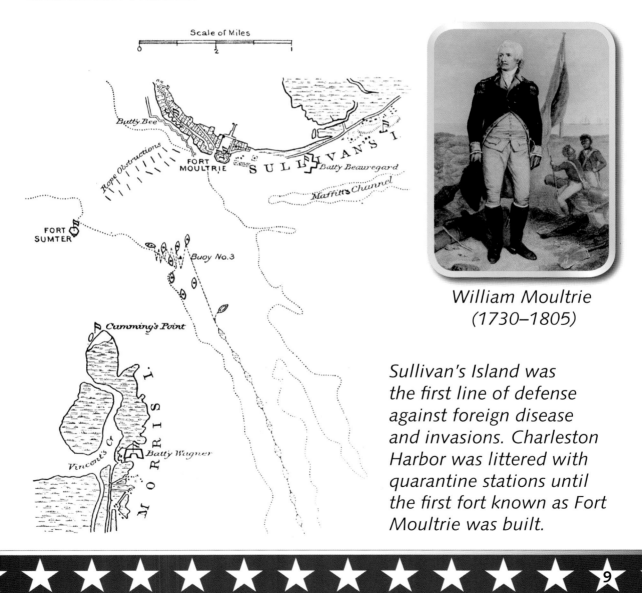

William Moultrie
(1730–1805)

Sullivan's Island was the first line of defense against foreign disease and invasions. Charleston Harbor was littered with quarantine stations until the first fort known as Fort Moultrie was built.

Work began on the new fort in 1829. The fort had five sides and measured 300 feet (91.4 meters) wide by 350 feet (106.7 meters) long. Its walls were five feet (1.5 meters) thick and about 40 feet (12.2 meters) tall. Platforms were built along the walls facing the harbor. These platforms were lined with guns so soldiers could defend the fort and the water around it. Inside the fort was an open area called a parade ground, where soldiers **drilled** and practiced. The soldiers lived in three buildings inside the safety of the fort's walls. The government named the fort after General Thomas Sumter, a man from South Carolina, who had fought during the Revolutionary War.

General Thomas Sumter
(1734–1832)

Work continued on Fort Sumter for more than thirty years. By December 1860 the fort still was not finished. Although the fort was built to hold 140 guns, only 48 were in place. But it didn't matter. The world was about to change, and Fort Sumter was about to become the center of a new war.

Freedom Fact!

There wasn't enough land in the harbor to build a fort, so engineers brought in stone blocks to build a small island where the fort would stand.

Fort Sumter had plenty of room for soldiers to live and work. The thick walls protected the fort from gunfire.

Chapter 3

SIEGE!

After Abraham Lincoln was elected president in November of 1860, it soon became clear that the southern states were going to leave the **Union**. On December 20, 1860, South Carolina became the first state to secede.

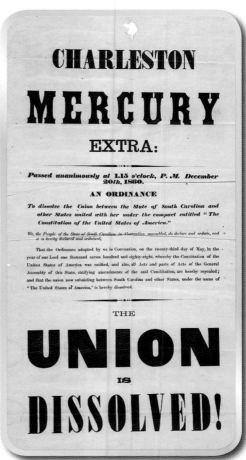

The flag that flies over the state of South Carolina today is of the same design that flew over the independent South Carolina during the Civil War.

A South Carolina newspaper announces the state has left the Union. Ten more states would follow in the next six months.

When South Carolina seceded, Union troops under Major Robert Anderson were stationed at Fort Moultrie. On December 24, South Carolina's governor, Francis Pickens sent letters to the federal government in Washington to discuss what would be done with U.S. forts in the South. Before Pickens received an answer, Major Anderson jumped into action. On December 26, Anderson and his men destroyed Fort Moultrie and left in the middle of the night to sail to Fort Sumter. Even though it was unfinished, Fort Sumter was easier to defend than Fort Moultrie.

Francis Pickens
(1805–1869)

The people of Charleston were very angry when they found out what Major Anderson had done. Governor Pickens sent troops to surround Fort Sumter. When a ship filled with supplies arrived from New York on January 9, 1861, Pickens' men fired on it before it could reach the fort. Anderson watched as the ship, filled with much-needed food and supplies, was forced to turn away.

Two days later, Pickens demanded that Anderson surrender the fort. Anderson refused, even though the fort was running low on food. Pickens knew Anderson needed food, and he sent some to the fort a few days later. However, Anderson refused to accept it. Soon afterward, Pickens allowed forty-five women and children to leave the fort. Then Anderson and his soldiers settled in to wait.

Major Robert Anderson

Major Anderson was sent to Charleston to protect all federal property. Shortly after his arrival, South Carolina seceded from the Union. Major Anderson moved his men from Fort Moultrie to the unfinished Fort Sumter. He and his men held down the fort until food and supplies ran out. His decision to move propelled the first shot of the Civil War.

Major Robert Anderson (1805–1871)

Ships from New York carrying much needed food and supplies could not enter the harbor during the ongoing bombardment of Fort Sumter. Without food and supplies, Major Anderson would have to surrender.

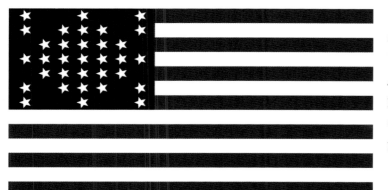

This flag design flew over Fort Sumter from April 12-14, 1861. Major Robert Anderson lowered the flag when the fort fell to Confederate forces during the Civil War.

On March 1, Brigadier General P.G.T. Beauregard arrived in Charleston. The Confederate president, Jefferson Davis, had appointed Beauregard to command the military in Charleston. Beauregard quickly set to work setting up guns and other defenses around Fort Sumter.

President Lincoln took office on March 4. After his **inauguration**, he sent officials to Charleston to get information on the situation there. Those officials reported that Anderson would run out of food by the middle of April. Anderson had asked the government for more food, supplies, and weapons several times. Finally, on April 8, Anderson received a letter from the government saying a relief ship was on its way. Whether the ship would be allowed into the fort was another question.

Beauregard had no intention of letting supplies get to the fort. Beauregard sent more soldiers to guard the area around the fort, and he sent another demand for Anderson to surrender. Once again, Anderson refused.

Volunteers and soldiers outside the Charleston Hotel awaiting remarks from Confederate General Samuel McGowan.

General P.G.T. Beauregard

General Beauregard had much respect for Major Anderson. Beauregard had been Anderson's student at West Point. The two corresponded several times during the siege of Fort Sumter. Beauregard politely requested Anderson to surrender and even informed him as to when the Confederates would fire upon Fort Sumter.

Brigadier General P.G.T. Beauregard (1818–1893)

Located in New York, West Point is the United States Military Academy that has been training and educating future military leaders for over 200 years.

Chapter 4

ATTACK ON FORT SUMTER

It was about 4:30 on the morning of April 12, 1861, when **Confederate** troops opened fire on Fort Sumter. The first shots of the Civil War had been fired.

Inside the fort, Major Anderson held back. He did not want to use his limited supply of **ammunition** right away. Finally, just before 7:00 a.m., Captain Abner Doubleday fired the first return shots. The firing went on all morning. To protect his men, Anderson only had them fire guns from the lower part of the fort, which offered better protection.

Although the **bombardment** died down during the night, it started up again the next morning. Along with the gunfire, Major Anderson had another problem. Some of the Confederate shells were heated, and these "hot shots" set fire to the **barracks** where soldiers lived inside the fort.

Captain Abner Doubleday
(1819–1893)

Although outnumbered and low on ammunition, the Union forces did their best to fight off the southern attack on the fort.

Early in the afternoon of April 13, the staff holding the American flag over the fort was shot away. Anderson quickly raised the flag again, but the fallen flag made one of Beauregard's aides wonder what was really going on. Without getting permission from Beauregard, the aide rowed out to the fort and asked if Anderson was ready to surrender. Anderson said no but eventually agreed to surrender the fort. The white flag was raised later that afternoon.

This time, Beauregard saw the white flag and sent some of his aides to the fort to find out what was going on. Anderson agreed to officially surrender the fort at noon the next day, April 14.

Fort Sumter's surrender was a huge occasion. The people of Charleston filled the harbor with boats to see the big event. They cheered as Anderson turned the fort over to Beauregard. Then Anderson and his men climbed into boats and sailed away to two relief ships waiting in the harbor.

Freedom Fact!

Although several soldiers were injured during the attack on Fort Sumter, none were killed. However, two Union soldiers died when Anderson fired a one-hundred-gun salute as he lowered the American flag over the fort. One of the guns went off too early, killing two soldiers.

The Union viewed the attack on Fort Sumter as an act of war. The next day, April 15, President Lincoln called for 75,000 volunteers. The Civil War had begun.

Many towns and cities put up posters like this one to recruit soldiers to fight in the Civil War.

Freedom Fact!

Lincoln only asked those first volunteers for ninety days of service. Everyone believed the war would be over quickly. However, the Civil War would drag on for four years.

Chapter 5

THE UNION RETURNS

As soon as Major Anderson left Fort Sumter, Confederate forces poured in. The fort belonged to them now. They raised the Confederate flag over the fort. Then they repaired the damage from the attack. They made the fort stronger by adding sand and bags of cotton to the inside walls. More guns were added to the fort as well.

The Confederate flag being raised after the surrender of Fort Sumter by the Union Army.

About five hundred soldiers settled into life at Fort Sumter. Along with making repairs, they drilled on the parade ground. They cleaned and polished the ninety-five guns and made sure they worked correctly.

Because of Fort Sumter, Fort Moultrie, and other forts in the harbor, Charleston was very well-protected during the Civil War. For most of the next four years, the people of the city went about their business without any danger of a Union attack.

Charleston did not suffer much damage until the end of the Civil War. Then, in February 1865, Union forces captured the city.

The Union was determined to take Fort Sumter back. However, the first two years of the Civil War were fought in other parts of the country. Finally, in April 1863, Union forces returned to Charleston Harbor. It was time to try to take back Fort Sumter.

The first attempt to take back Fort Sumter came from the water. The Union sent ships to fire on the fort. These ships were called **ironclads** because they were covered with iron for protection. For two-and-a-half hours, the ironclads fired at the fort, while the Confederates fired back with their cannons. The Confederates fired more than 2,000 shots compared to just 154 shots from the Union ships. The attack on the fort failed.

The Union created a new plan after the first failed attempt. They would attack Fort Sumter from land and sea. As ships bombarded the fort from the harbor, Union guns shot thousands of shells at the fort from nearby Morris Island. Fort Sumter was heavily damaged, its walls broken by cannon fire, but its soldiers refused to surrender.

Despite firing thousands of shells at the fort in 1863, Union forces were not able to recapture Fort Sumter.

The battle to retake Fort Sumter went on for 22 long months. The Union fired more than seven million pounds of ammunition at the fort. Still, the fort did not fall. Finally, on February 17,1865, a large Union army approached Charleston from Savannah, Georgia. The Confederates knew they were beaten, and they left the fort. Once again, Fort Sumter was under Union control.

On April 14, 1865, Major Robert Anderson returned to Fort Sumter. He raised the Union flag over the ruins of the fort.

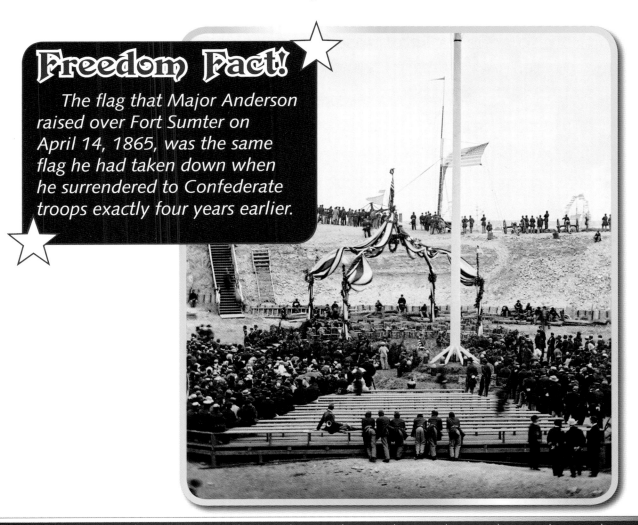

Freedom Fact!

The flag that Major Anderson raised over Fort Sumter on April 14, 1865, was the same flag he had taken down when he surrendered to Confederate troops exactly four years earlier.

Chapter 6

AFTER THE WAR

Fort Sumter continued to serve as an American fort after the Civil War ended. In 1865 the United States Army repaired the fort. It also added a lighthouse in order to guide ships coming into the harbor.

During the Spanish-American War in 1898, the U.S. Army built a gun **battery** at the fort and added long-range guns. However, these guns were never fired in battle. Soldiers and guns were stationed at the fort during World War I (1914–1918) and World War II (1939–1945), but no shots were ever fired and the fort was never attacked.

In 1948 the United States made Fort Sumter a national monument. The National Park Service takes care of the fort. Visitors arrive at the fort by boat from Charleston. Once at the fort, they can walk over several acres and see many Civil War guns and cannonballs. National Park Service rangers are also on the island to give talks and demonstrations to bring the Civil War and other important facts of American history to life.

Tourists at Fort Sumter can see some of the flags that flew over the fort during the Civil War.

Fort Sumter has been part of United States history for more than two hundred years. From its position in one of America's most important harbors, it saw the first shots of the war that divided our country. Today we can visit Fort Sumter to learn more about that war and this important symbol of our freedom.

Freedom Fact!

More than 300,000 people visit Fort Sumter every year.

TIMELINE

1776 —— *Fort Moultrie is built on Sullivan's Island.*

1798 —— *Fort Moultrie is rebuilt.*

1804 —— *Fort Moultrie is destroyed in a hurricane.*

1811 —— *Fort Moultrie is rebuilt again.*

1829 —— *Construction begins on Fort Sumter.*

1860 —— *South Carolina secedes from the Union.*

1860 —— *U.S. Army Major Robert Anderson moves his men from Fort Moultrie to Fort Sumter.*

1861 —— *The Confederates under Brigadier General P.G.T. Beauregard bombard Fort Sumter in the first shots of the Civil War.*

1861 —— *Anderson surrenders Fort Sumter to the Confederates.*

1863 —— *The Union begins a twenty-two-month bombardment of Fort Sumter.*

1865 —— *Confederates abandon Fort Sumter.*

1865 —— *Major Anderson raises the U.S. flag over the fort.*

1898 —— *A gun battery and long-range guns are added to Fort Sumter.*

1914–1918 *Fort Sumter is manned during World War I, but no shots are fired.*

1939–1945 *Fort Sumter is manned during World War II, but no shots are fired.*

1948 —— *Fort Sumter becomes a national monument.*

GLOSSARY

ammunition (am-yuh-NISH-uhn): objects such as bullets or shells fired from weapons

barracks (BAR-iks): buildings where soldiers live

battery (BA-tuh-ree): a group of guns

bombardment (bom-BARD-ment): an attack with large guns, such as cannons

Confederate (con-FEH-duh-ret): having to do with the eleven southern states that seceded from the United States

drilled (DRILLED): practiced by doing something over and over again

federal (FED-ur-uhl): having to do with the central power of a country

inauguration (in-aw-gyuh-RAY-shuhn): the ceremony of swearing in a president or public official

ironclads (EYE-urn-kladz): ships covered with iron or steel for protection

plantations (plan-TAY-shuhnz): large farms found in warm climates

seceded (suh-SEED-ed): left a country to form a separate nation

Union (YOON-yuhn): the United States of America

INDEX

SHOW WHAT YOU KNOW

1. Why did the South need slaves and the North did not?
2. Was President Lincoln for or against slavery?
3. In what year did Fort Sumter become a national monument.
4. How long was the battle to retake Fort Sumter?
5. How many soldiers were injured during the attack on Fort Sumter?

WEBSITES TO VISIT

www.historynet.com/battle-of-fort-sumter
www.ducksters.com/history/battle_of_fort_sumter.php
www.civilwar.org/battlefields/fort-sumter.html

ABOUT THE AUTHOR

Joanne Mattern has written hundreds of books for children. Her favorite subjects are history, nature, sports, and biographies. She enjoys traveling around the United States and visiting new places. Joanne grew up on the banks of the Hudson River and still lives in the area with her husband, four children, and numerous pets.

Meet The Author!
www.meetREMauthors.com

PHOTO CREDITS: Cover © ; Title Page © John Wollworth; page 5, 24 © Duncan P. Walker; page 6 © photolibrary.com; page 7 © Rainer Lesniewski, Library of congress; page 8 © Lori Skelton; page 9, 10, 12, 13, 14, 17, 19, 21, 23, 25 © wikipedia; page 11, 15, 19, 22, 27 © Library of Congress; page 12 © noriworld, page 15 © Devin Cook/Wikipedia; page 16 © Craig McCausland; page 17 © American Sprint; page 28 © Gabrielle Hovey

Edited by: Luana Mitten

Cover design by: Renee Brady
Interior design by: Rhea Magaro

Library of Congress PCN Data

Fort Sumter / Joanne Mattern
(Symbols of Freedom)
ISBN 978-1-63430-046-9 (hard cover)
ISBN 978-1-63430-076-6 (soft cover)
ISBN 978-1-63430-105-3 (e-Book)
Library of Congress Control Number: 2014953367

Printed in the United States of America, North Mankato, Minnesota

Also Available as:

ROURKE'S
e-Books